Advance Praise for Buddha and Biryani

Here is a collection of poems that mostly deromanticize the world through irony and black humour. The poet distances himself from what he sees to make his observation sharper and clearer. Ra Sh finds poetry in everything from microbes to machines and mountains. There are moments of silent anguish as when the poet remembers his mother though he never waxes sentimental as most poets do on such occasions. I have seldom seen poets using repetition so skilfully, each refrain adding weight to the earlier one as in the opening poems — "Silent Farewells," "Last Global Warning," and "Why is this Damn River in a Hurry," "A List of Signboards the Flood Left Behind" are fine examples of Ra Sh's kind of sarcasm. While you expect a poem on evanescence, he gives you a poem on our cherished vanities and beliefs that the flood refuses to recognize. "Buddha and Biryani," the title poem, is about desire — the desire for good food — that even the Buddha's dispassion fails to conquer. Gods, ghosts, ghouls, black magicians, and mythological characters parade these poems with ease as they are shorn of their loads of men's faith in them, and even sex turns into a tantalizing, even cannibalistic,  ritual.

— K. SATCHIDANANDAN

# BUDDHA and BIRYANI

*poems*

RA SH

Hawakal
PUBLISHERS

New Delhi | Calcutta

**HAWAKAL**
New Delhi | Calcutta

HAWAKAL PUBLISHERS PRIVATE LIMITED
70 B/9 Amritpuri, East of Kailash, New Delhi 65
33/1/2 K B Sarani, Mall Road, Calcutta 80

Email info@hawakal.com
Website www.hawakal.com

Cover designed by Bitan Chakraborty

First edition (paperback) September 2022



ISBN: 978-93-91431-02-0 (paperback)

Price: INR 350 | USD 15.99

*for*
my Mother
who is no more

# INTRODUCTION

Now that I am five-poetry-book-deep, it is time for resurfacing for air and ruminating about the dive lying on the warm volcanic rocks. Let my thoughts be in dark shades. I am returning to the beginning in more senses than one. The poems in the anthology, *A Strange Place Other Than Ear Lobes*, which came out seven years back (out of print), celebrated battered flesh and spattered blood like in a butcher shop. The body was the beginning and end without a soul in sight. Some of those poems have trickled down here.

The first collection, *Architecture Of Flesh*, was a mixed baggage crammed with poems on love, language, sexuality, and politics. Even the most erotic of those poems had an anti-state/anti-public opinion flavor which boomed into a anti-fascist explosion. *The Bullet Train*, my second collection, was political to the core. I had to take a breather then and think about love and only love, as a sort of retribution, in its various manifestations like multi-limped goddesses. To return to love is like connecting my lungs to an oxygen cylinder. Love is what keeps me going. It is my driving force, my energy source. Thus were born two completely different books on love, *Kintsugi by Hadni*, with phantasmagorical visions of love and, in opposition to it, lyrical love in the chapbook I wrote with Ritamvara Bhattacharya, *In The Mirror, Our Graves*. One showed unbridled passion and eroticism, while the other was ethereal — timeless, ageless, genderless love.

Like I said in the beginning, all these have come back in body-bags this time, with many poems on death, farewells, post-pandemic dystopia, hope, and hopelessness. So this is the fare I am offering this time.

*Buddha and Biryani* will move readers constantly through the dark and dampness of the catacombs underneath the known world, pushing further and further into the darkness until they hit a rare bright spot. The journey of farewells which started with a violin ends with the strains of the Dranyen, a Tibetan musical instrument. This collection is a wail or a dirge, mourning who else but the poet!

**Ra Sh**
4 Aug 2022

# Contents


Silent Farewells 11
Last Global Warning 12
Why Is This Damn River In A Hurry 13
A List Of Signboards That The Flood Left Behind 14
Surival Kit 17
The City Of The Blind 18
X-Mom 19
Umbilical Ache 20
Doodling Absence 21
Grand Mammaries 23
Grand Magician 25
Occult 27
The Suicide Bathers 28
Buddha And Biryani 29
The Rain Within 31
While We Wait For The Other 32
Nemesis – Stellar Journey 33
Blurring The 'Ing' 35
Butcher Girl 1 36
Butcher Girl 2 38
Skin Poem 40
Ezhimala/Comala 41
Fire Air 43
Ethyl Dreams 45
Ram Aur Shyam 46
Oh...These Kisans! 48
Three Pellets And A Cradle 50
A Series In 4 Episodes 52
Some Pious Deeds 54
The Somnambulist 56
Minnal Maniyan 58

Mullai And Palai                                          59
Return Of The Seeds                                      60
The Luminous Seed                                        61
Where, In What Form, Shall We Meet Again?                63
My Tea                                                    64
A Couple Burning From Love                               66
Last Love                                                 67
Break Up                                                  68
The Mortuary Wars                                        69
Sunsrt Rape in Languid Hills                             70
Why Did You Rape Me?                                     71
End Of The Sex War                                       73
Ms Tiny Tits                                              75
She And Shemale                                           76
Ode To An Unsending Girl                                 78
A Desperate Straight Man's Lament                        80
Love In The Time Of The Karuna Virus                     82
A Jatka In The Night                                     84
Two Covid-19 Viruses Meet Albert Camus                   86
Pathology Of A Rainbow                                   88
Contemporary Bacteria                                    90
Death Of An Inflammable Woman                            92
Many A Time                                               93
Narcissus Does The Mirror Act                            94
On Photography                                            95
Sound Bites                                               96
The First Syllable                                       97
The Ex-Communists Or Exorcised Communists, A Farce       99
The Russian Predator                                    101
Obituary To A Man In Hurry                              102
The Fallen Condom – A Condomporary Musical Tragedy      104
Ode To Black Holes                                      106
The Unbearable Yellowness Of Yellow Deaths              107
Dranyen                                                  108

## SILENT FAREWELLS

When things start leaving you
they don't say bye.
Silently, they leave in a row.

My dad did not say bye
when he died.
My mom did not say bye
when she died.

My house did not say bye
when it quietly collapsed.
My garden did not say bye
when it went under water.

Finally, my love my love
my love did not say bye
when she left
when she left.

When I left me
I left quietly
leaving no trail of good byes.
But I heard a violin from afar.


Note: This poem got 114 translations in Malayalam, 21 in Indan languages
and 7 in international languages

## LAST GLOBAL WARNING

Dear sluggish earthworm
don't burrow the earth
You may be cemented.

Dear sprightly grasshopper
don't hop around in vain
You may be skewered.

Dear shiny loony moon
don't show your bright face
You may be eclipsed.

Dear sweet mynah
don't sing so loud
Your voice may be severed.

Dear green peacock
don't dance in public
You may be maimed.

Dear little sparrow
don't get raped
You could be jailed

Dear distant pole star
don't show us the way.
You may be blinded.

Your genocide is on its way.
Your terminator has landed.
He works alphabetically.

# WHY IS THIS DAMN RIVER IN A HURRY

Why is this damn river
in tearing hurry to reach the sea?
Why is that giant teak tree
uprooting its roots one by one
to leap into that river?
Why are the birds roosting on the tree
leaving their nests
to fly with the storm?

Why is everything everyone bound for the sea?
Why the planes trains cars ships
why the cattle lions camels rats
why the men women kids bodies
why the bridges houses malls toilets
why the temples mosques churches graves
why the ploughs tractors threshers sickles
why the channels news studios vans
why the parliaments forts moats sewers
why the rifles guns cannons tanks
why the roads parks theatres slums
why is everything everyone bound for the sea?

Why fire air ether earth
why skin blood semen eggs
why is everything drowning in the sea?
Why the sea is swallowing the sea?
Why the sea sea sea sea?
Why the sea frothing sea?
Why the sea?

## A LIST OF SIGNBOARDS THAT
## THE FLOOD LEFT BEHIND

1

No entry for Non-Hindus

The copper plated roof of the seven hundred
year old temple struggled briefly for air
before going down. Hindu bubbles kept floating
to the surface till a boat named Daivasahayam reached
and moored itself to the flag post.

2

Beware of the Dog.

The German shepherd in the kennel
could not break the gate open,
but a pack of mongrels had
made the roof their home and
knew how to howl when
the choppers approached.

3

Get appointment first.

The man attired in a suit
wearing black leather shoes

was stuck under the staircase
visiting card in hand.

4

Trespassers will be prosecuted

When the owners returned
apart from clay and weeds
they found a cobra and a viper
in the prayer room and the
yoga room.

5

This is not a public road.

Two large fishing boats
failed to enter the narrow private road.
Finally, a *meen vallam* with five men aboard
negotiated the walls and gates
to release twenty trapped souls.

6

Today's prices.

A row of ten dead kids
lay under the board,
one of them still in a
uniform wearing a badge.

7

Instructions about clothes to wear while worshiping

The heap of clothes that

reached in a pick up truck
were of various sizes and brands
smelling of dead water and not incense.

8

Begging is prohibited

They begged for life
on a top floor balcony
to the wind and the rain
and the distant thunder of
helicopters surveying aerially.
Their voices went unheard
even to the bare bodied black men
in the rowing boats.

9

Pay and Use toilet

They used nature
as a toy for them to play
and push aside.
They paid for it much later.

Note: Based on the flood situation in Kerala
Meen Vallam – country boat for fishing
with inputs from Rajesh Nandiyode, Malayalam poet

## SURIVAL KIT

Know this to survive.
You can return to the place you left
not the place that left you.

You may go hiking
but never find it.
You may hitch up a peak
to find it was the wrong peak.
You will begin the climb
to know you forgot the oxygen
and the ice axe.

Same time, the oxygen
and the axe may be looking for you.
All the three are destined
never to meet.

However equipped you are to survive
life still eludes you.
You go on a hide and seek game
which you are not good at.
And survival depends on
how you find you.

Such are your thoughts
when you gulp down
the piping hot masala chai
at Giani Da Dabha
in the valley before the ascent.

Exactly 40 minutes before
your bus overturns.

# THE CITY OF THE BLIND

In the city of the blind
I found kids playing
blind man's buff.

I played and lost
the blinds melted away
soon as I covered my eyes.

A kid explained to me.
where light is unwanted
the sun never rises.
Eyes are only dark pools
where black lotuses bloom.

In the city of the blind
you dont find what you find
unless they are placed there
for you not to find.

Next time I covered my eyes
I saw black rivers, soot hills,
ashen trees and shadowy kids.

With a woman sculpted in coal
I walked blind folded
to the city of light.
The sun died forever
before we reached.

# X-MOM
*for my mom who died in 2018*

Mom had two hearts like two breasts.
One of stone and
one of flesh.
They worked alternatively.

On days when the pulpy one worked
she talked of my infantile jaundice days
when I turned turmeric yellow.
I would have died but for a doctor
named Adam Khan in *Pazhavangadi*. (1)

On days when the stony heart worked
she slept with a *koduval* under her pillow (2)
to protect us kids from potential enemies.

Till she died, she maintained
"A woman should always carry
a hack knife in her heart."

On the night of her death,
I found it glowing in the dark
on an X-ray shot of her chest.


(1)      A place in Trivandrum, Kerala. We lived there in 57-62.
(2)      Hack knife.

## UMBILICAL ACHE

The crow did land, *amma*,
on my belly and pecked
at my navel devoid of a
beginning and end like a
lotus hanging rootless.

You nourished me through
this non-existent tube for
sixty two years feeding me
with memories and fables
and tales of other mothers.

It does hurt when your
volatile history clashes
with my mild passive one
without teeth and claws
to fight this fearsome world.

Souls go food-less, eyes open
on dark walls, ears crammed
with the screams of the
innocent, people numbered
in a register, tears in dust bins.

Yes amma, feed on my blood,
dance on my entrails, tear
asunder my flesh, claim your
right to teach me how to fight,
lay a new egg in our lost nest
to hatch me afresh to caw in
a thousand new languages.

Note: *amma* – mother

## DOODLING ABSENCE

Early in the morning there was no hiss of the
water filling the tank.
There was no hum from the washing machine.
The cat did not mew or jump down from the attic.

When the woman went out to sweep, a crow sat
on a branch and watched her uncawing.
Two squirrels sat on another branch unchirping.
Two street dogs who usually pay a visit for leftovers
sat on the compound wall unnbarking.

They all looked at her sadly.

The flowers all withered and dropped dead on
the ground.
Two newspapers lay dead near the
front door.
The mixie switched iself on with a loud wail and
abruptly stopped.
The burner spluttered in sorrow while boiling milk.
The cooker refused to whistle.
The geyser refused to turn on.

When the woman brought tea to the man, he was
struggling with the TV. Grainy heads appeared
one after the other looking for the absent kid.
His phone screen lit up with a single msg. Where is she?

The msg began to repeat itself in all languages.
The dead land phone began to ring incessantly.

Far away a kid screamed refusing to go to school.
She sat down on a chair and started doodling the
figures of an old man and a woman.

Huge tears sprang comically from their eyes.

## GRAND MAMMARIES

My grandma was the first woman
to be part of the newly built road.

She had only one milch cow.
A calf. (I took them grazing!)
Four five hens that laid eggs for us.
Boiled egg and milk rice was our staple
diet. Her dad our grand grandad was
an occult man who grew saplings from
just planted seeds. He gave us ripe
mangoes from those trees.

One night, he lay dead
on a field,  beaten by an *odiyan*.

I learnt milking cows from her.
How to smear butter on the udders before
milking. Milk vending machines came
much later in life when I went to a
city. She taught us many things magical
and scary like love.

When an arrack shop opened right across
the road, she frequented the shop for a
100 every noon. I sat looking at the news-
paper  when she drank.

A new metal road was being laid.
One day, a lorry pasted an image of her on the road.
When she died, magic died.

We became addicted to gadgets. Grand-
ma became a witch on a broom.
Grand grand dad, the wizard, became
the wizard of oz.

Note: *Odiyan* — A Demon Who Could Change His form at will

## GRAND MAGICIAN

In the bamboo grove, I heard such
strange noises and voices  and screams
that I fell to the ground, stunned.

Kids were not allowed to pass through
that grove guarded by ghouls..

When I came to my senses, I found
my grandpa mumbling some chants
over me.

I watched as he took a square copper
sheet and scrawled many figures on them
while praying.

It was slipped into a cylinder and sealed
with wax and tied round my waist.
I carried that amulet throughout my life.

When a lightning struck, all people in the
bus shelter died, except me.
When our train collided with another,
all people in the compartment died,
except me.
Following a change of management,
all my colleagues were laid off,
except me.

Jilted by their lovers, all my old friends
committed suicide,
except me.

Yesterday night, I found my dead grandpa
silently untying my amulet and
vanishing with a smile.

And, from today I have become a
non-citizen
with no proof of identity.

## Occult

Before the occult ritual
he drew the red from hyacinths
green from the curry leaves
yellow from the turmeric
and blue from the bowl of ocean
kept in his secret cave.

This is not me, he said
to the frightened bronze mirror.
This is my great grandpa
in search of Ghouls and *Odiyans*.

He did not return that night.
His body lay on a paddy field
drained of all colours.
*Maadan* was covering his own face
with hyacinths, curry leaves, turmeric
and a splash of ocean.

Note: *Maadan* and *Odiyan* are demi-Gods of the dalits. *Odiyan* is known for sorcery

# THE SUICIDE BATHERS

The water muddy rose like brown globules
of blood on the lotus infested east *kadavu*.
As I sank naked I saw a pair of eyes in the
water weeds. Slowly, eyes began to sparkle
in pairs from all around. I looked away from
them towards the women bathing in the
north *kadavu*.

The noons always found the pond quiet, in siesta,
dreaming of the monsoon. The noons always found
the women swimming half naked their legs thrashing.
The noons always found the drowned women rise
with swaying hair to the surface.

Father warned me people warned me, don't go to
the pond in the noons.

I found my playmates there. Making love underwater
to dead women. The fish hovered above us, a water snake,
some frogs, a few turtles, and many bangled hands.

When I surfaced hours later in the north *kadavu*
the women were gone and the washing stones were silent.
I always walked home naked, pausing under the palms,
with a stem of lotus between my teeth.

To return to many more noons
and drowned women in ecstasy free from bonds.

Note: Kadavu – Assigned spots in the pond for bathing

## BUDDHA AND BIRYANI

When Buddha awoke from
his psychotropic trance,
the analyst who had hypnotized him
asked, "How do you feel now Lord?
Are you free from
the clutches of Karma?"


Before replying,
Buddha's nostrils flared.
He asked, "What's that
heavenly scent assailing
my senses?"


The Psycho sniffed the air
like a police dog and said,
"That's Biryani, my Lord!"


The famished Lord said,
"Ah! Let me taste some of that
heavenly stuff before exiting
this damn cycle of food and feces."


In gastronomic fervor,
the Lord transmigrated
on a long foodie trip
to all parts of the globe.

He relished Biryani with
Saji Kabab in Kabul,
Yak wraps in Lhasa,
Kukul Mas curry in Colombo,
Shabu-shabu in China,
Seollangtang in Korea,
Gyu Kushi in Japan,
Phat kaphrao in Thailand,
Amok trey in Cambodia,
Nwa Mee Hinga in Myanmar.


Satiated and saliva dripping
from his inflamed tongue
he lay down to sleep in a
grove of Sala trees after a meal of pork
offered by a blacksmith.


In delirium, he dreamt of
partaking Daal Bhat Tarkari
In the kitchen of Yasodhara,
then nine months pregnant.
He attained Parinirvana
in his gastro enteric slumber.


Wherever he had eaten,
his faith spread
as he had commanded
his disciples to eat
whatever they got as alms
from the people.


Therefore, Ananda,
in the cycle of life and death,
there is no right food
or wrong food.
The cannibals know that best.

# THE RAIN WITHIN

What streams within
pours within
gushes within
is a rain within a rain.
A hot stream spurting
from the frozen river.

Doors are shivering
trees are trembling.
moon is screaming.
The rain that lashes
the wilderness within
lacerates the ventricles
like sharp edges of icicles.

When a lover's heart shatters
rubies and pearls tumble out,
the rain falls on a steaming reef
soothing the embers sputtering.

Her figure fades in sans umbrella
in the downpour watching you
hair simmering in the lightning
nude naked unclad unrobed.

When you drag yourself
towards the unattainable one
rain ceases around you and her
in two rainless circles closing in
around whom like a cylinder rise
the boughs the nests the broken eggs.

# WHILE WE WAIT FOR THE OTHER

While we wait for the Other
the sea evaporates shore to shore
One shore burns like lava
the other crystallizes like ice.


A coil of seaweed floats dead.
A sunflower turns to the moon.
The earth is a glazed glass painting.
Trees whisper horrors of the past.
The wishing well runs dry.
Skylarks peck at hot pebbles.
A peak vanishes from the bare hill.
A jill and a jack drop down a hole.
A row of cars explode one by one.
It rains shoes and severed heels.


The land twists on its axis.
The river rolls on its back.

While we wait for the Other.

## NEMESIS – STELLAR JOURNEY

On one of my stellar journeys
hopping from globe to globe
like a celestial toad,
I met Nemesis again
starbathing on an asteroid headed
for the edge of the universe, humming
a humma humma.

She swooped down on me like
a flying serpent and shouted across
the vacuum, hey, poet, care for some toxins?

Before I could say angel, she pulled out a boob
and squirted some into my gaping mouth,
that's how  I came to be known
as a poet blue in this century.

She had three breasts,
one oozing images, one words
and one some anatacid antiflatulent demulcent.
She was cyanide on the move.
She had just poisoned Narcissus to death,
raped Zeus and was banished as an
evil star on sun's far orbit.

On my way back to earth after winning a
billion dollar poetry prize, I visited her evil star

and her tomb marked with three conical pyramids.
She had left a sex doll for me tagged
`from your Nemesis' and a bottle of clear
water from the Oceanus and a clip recording the
squeals of the male god as she buggered him
with a stylus.

Note: Nemesis was the child of Oceanus, the river-ocean that covered
earth before the formation of land masses. Nemesis killed Narcissus.
Nemesis mated with Zeus,the supreme God.

From the anthology, *A Strange Place Other Than Earlobes*

## BLURRING THE 'ING'

Your nose ring sparkling
like a sweat drop murmuring
on your lips fluttering.
Your ear rings ushering
new longings to your hearing.
The nipple rings chewing
at mammary nibblings.
The navel ring tinkering
with belly layerings.
Toe rings rippling.
Finger rings fumbling.
Clit rings tingling.

Darling, you are ascending,
as the world is floundering
at the brink of collapsing,
warring, suffering, oppressing,
flickering, glikering, hicklering,
bewildering butchering torturing
fuhrer-ring, tringering ing ing ing

Come abilfezomonaxing!


Note: From the anthology, *A Strange Place Other Than Earlobes*

## BUTCHER GIRL 1

Like a slab of putrefying meat, I
lie supinely on the cold slab, waiting
for the Butcher Girl, my queen, my
gallows, my guillotine, my gory death.

Do the dead sleep, but I do, a
moment of stupor, a wink, and the
Butcher Girl emerges, in full splendour, she is
on me, above me, atop me, amazon-ly.

In immortal fear, I hear her laugh like a
cracking storm, a volcanic fusillade, see
her sap-slurping lips, her chomping
teeth, her forked tongue.

She, the queen of the nether world, my
butcher, her hair coiled with mating
serpents, eyes flashing grasshopper green, nostrils
screwed with gleaming metal springs, her nakedness
riveted with studs, rings, balls, coils,
blades, spokes, on her boobs, belly, bum,
cunt, sighing thighs.

She grimaces at my long dead face and lets
out a shriek of ecstasy and makes
love to me organ by organ

with the quickness of a spider.
In her several limbs, she brandishes the
weapons of my undoing -
flay knives, bone tongs, clamps,

choppers, backsaws, tenderizers,
machetes, hammers, sharp-cutters,
rods, rippers, bone-crunchers,
grinders, slicers, extractors -
setting a frenetic pace of dismantlement,
dismemberment, demolition, deconstruction.

Till, on that cold slab of death, nothing
remains, but she and me. She sheaths
her weapons, rests her limbs and
secretes a serenading smile and
beckons me to be
with her and
I do.

Note: From the anthology, *A Strange Place Other Than Earlobes*

## Butcher Girl 2

Like a slab of putrefying text, I
lie supine on a frozen sheet, waiting
for the Butcher Girl, the semantic queen, the
universal grammar girl, the pedagogue, the
lexical abecedary.

In diabolic fear, I hear her laugh like a
vicarious storm, a volcanic fusillade, see
her word-slurping lips, her chomping
teeth designed for the bony allusions,
her forked syntactic tongue.

She, the queen of the semiotic world,
her nakedness riveted with grammatical
morphemes,idioms, allegories,
oxymorons,syllables,
metaphors,alliterations
and dreaded punctuation.

She grimaces at my dying text and lets
out a shriek of ecstasy and begins the war
with the quickness of a spider.

In her multi-limbs, she brandishes the
weapons of my text's undoing –
roland barthes flay knives umberto eco bone tongs
jürgen habermas backsaws jean baudrillard bone-crunchers

jacques derrida sharp cutters gilles deleuze rippers
jacques lacan  extractors  judith butler grinders and
michel foucault machetes and hammers.
Setting a frenetic pace of dismantlement,
dismemberment, demolition, deconstruction.

Till, on that cold slab of death, nothing
remains, but she and  my text
on palm leaves cut in  rectangular strips
on which are scrawled some  runes
in my language that signify my life and  ruin.

From the anthology, *A Strange Place Other Than Earlobes*

## Skin poem

What will you sketch on my skin when
I am dead, I asked her? She said, cheerfully –

On your brow I will draw a dry well. On your
cheeks twin horns of a sterile bull. On your nose
an abandoned chimney. Around your mouth, ha ha,
an anus red with lipstick. Around your neck a fiber green
snake swallowing its own tail.

Go on go on, I entreated her, now aroused. She said –
around your nipples I will draw a bow and arrow, around
your navel a snail, on your penis, she went on holding it gingerly, a
rusted cannon, on your eggs, she squeezed them gently, two empty
shells,
your thighs will feature an excavator and a mine shaft, knees
two wrecking balls, on your feet I will draw a shovel
and an axe. I came by then. I always do.

My back, my back, I pleaded, she said- turn over. I did.
She laughed and said, spanking me, on your bum I will design
two nuclear power plants. My back, my back, I cried
again. She said – I will rip off your skin and
write on it this poem, Damn You!

Note: From the anthology, *A Strange Place Other Than Earlobes*

## Ezhimala/Comala

I had a strange dream about a village of ghosts.
The village became active only in the night.
Ghosts gathered in the local arrack shop and drank.
They played cards.  Women ghosts joined them
and had fun. Strangely, there were ghosts falling in love
and a few extra and premarital relationships. You won't believe,
the ghosts could even fuck to draw out
only cries of ecstasy.
The ghosts were hardly bothered about food,
hunger, pangs of jealousy, changes in weather.
I thought of *Comala*, the village in *Pedro Parama*.

The very next day, we went on a trip to Ezhimala,
the future venue of the Ezhimala Naval Academy.
From the moment we crossed the border,
we found houses devoid of men, women,
kids, pets. The streets  empty. No electricity,
no televisions, radios.

The arrack shop had crumbled. We walked to the
beach and kept meeting silence after silence.
The wind, sometimes, blew like a marching song.
But, when we reached the beach, it was thickly  populated
with people who were engaged in the strangest of activities.
They hardly glanced at us. It was like an extended circus
on a stretch of white sand. There was an abandoned rusty ship
grounded in the sea to which people swam and back.

Some did cartwheels. Some stood around a bar-be-que.

Some were doing poetry performances.
Some sang Baburaj songs from the sixties rivaled by
another group that sang revolutionary songs.
You won't believe, there were even Leftists, Rightists
and Centrists among them. Some were drinking.

I dozed off.

I woke up with my head on the lap of a girl.
She was combing my hair.
We were the only two left on the sand.
I asked her where I was.
She said, "Comala!" We made love under a full moon.
We waxed and waned like the tides.

Days and years passed and we are still on the beach
making love whenever we feel like.
Meanwhile, a township has come up around us with
real people, dogs and cadets. Training centres and
signalling stations bristling with activity have also proliferated.
People are hanged to death regularly from raised anchors.
Once, we even witnessed a woman being raped by seven men,
skinned, flesh ripped out and bar-be-qued on the grill.

Enconsed in our parallel world, we know all this will
crumble one day, the township will be wiped out,
the base will vanish but the sand will
remain with us, two ghosts, making love.

Note:
Baburaj – a famous music composer in Kerala

# FIRE AIR

In 1770s, air was a mixture of fire air
and foul air, according to Sheele.
There were reservations about this fire air.
Priestly pompously called it the
dephlogisticated air.
Bored with these foul names,
Lavoisier called it Oxygen.*

In the 1970s, the wind blew
over our *perumkulam* and brought **
with it the scent of over ground trees
and underwater sea life.
It was all fire air, that set our nerves on fire,
charged us with an unending supply of
electric charges and energy boosters.
We saw oxygen not in the fire air
but in the chemistry lab where water
was electrolyzed to split it into H and O.
We saw the fire air captured in the tube.

In the 2020s, in a small city flat
obnoxious with foul air and no fire air
I have little oxygen cylinders that I keep refilling.
When I go out into the throng of poisonous gases
that sting my eyes and burn my nostrils,
I wear a mask and carry an Oxygen pack like
the Everest climbers and moon walkers.

The wind still blows over our *perumkulam*
bringing with it the scent of over ground trees
and under water sea life.
My body was burnt in Nigam Bodh Ghat***
but my spirit hangs around here.
Even we spirits need fire air to dance
and are not used to industrial Oxygen.

Note:

*The three scientists who identified Oxygen as a separate element.
**A large pond or tank used by villagers for bathing and irrigation.
***Biggest crematorium in Delhi by the banks of River Jamuna.

(Written at a time when the burning ghats could not manage the rows of
corona corpses.)

## ETHYL DREAMS

When I was an adolescent, all kinds of
sensations prickled me. One was my
unnatural attraction to my Chemistry
teacher, not to her face or her body
but the way she said 'E-t-h-y-l.'

The word coming from her mouth
aroused me like a blue bunsen flame.
The 'Thy' pretty near got me to climax.
Suddenly the scent of aldehydes spread
in the air and the multi coloued liquids
in the chemical shelf gleamed. A blob of
mercury ran up and down my member.

Even years later while pleasuring myself
I reserved the best part for her lips
brewing the word Ethyl alcohol.
It became so sensory that I began to use
Ethyl or Methyl to the same effect.
I urged her to say nonsensical words like
Bethyl, Fethyl, Zethyl, Rethyl or Lethyl.

I became an ethyl alcoholic, but cried
when she and her lips died with the
word 'Ethyl' on them. I am a teetotaller
now and lead a saintly life having lost
the power to Ethylify.

## Ram Aur Shyam

Farmers on tractors and
battalions behind barbed wire
shoot *nayi saal mubarak ho*
at the stroke of midnight
while nursing their injuries and
preparing for the first battle
of 2021.

Langars are aflame
with the heat of the protests
as women cook with men
for the foot soldiers of
revolution.
*Makki ki roti* and *sarson ka saag*
heal bodies and calm agitated minds.
The mechanic kids repair the wheels
of revolution the tractors and trucks
for the first battle of 2021.

Meanwhile with loads of laddoos and
tonnes of jalebis,  the powerful tweet
their greetings to the people
groveling in misery.

*Nayi saal mubaarak ho* echoes
from the corners of the country where
even citizenship is a delible mark on many.

"A cold wave sweeps North India" cries the papers.
In makeshift tents, *kisans* shiver in their blankets.
The fire from the *langar* and the heat from their crops
keep them warm in the *mandis* of power.

Ram, the *kisan* and
Shyam, the *jawan*
twins estranged at a global mela
stare at each other across the barricades.

Note: Ram aur Shyam – A typical Bollywood film in which two twins are lost
to each other in a festival gathering.
*Kisan* — farmer
*Jawan* — soldier
*Nayi saal mubarak ho* — happy new year
*Langars* — community kitchen
*Makki ki roti* — flat bread made from maize
*Sarsong ka sag* — a curry made from mustard leaves
*Mandis* — grain markets

The reference is to the struggle by Indian farmers against three Farm Bills
affecting them.

## OH...THESE KISANS!

These *kisans* are an ungracious lot.
What a bunch of ignorant fools!

We give them concessions.
They say they need rights.
We offer Ambani's bazaar.
They prefer *mandis*.
We offer Adani warehouses.
They prefer MSP.
We pass bills without asking.
They pass resolutions that jolt us.
We praise *kisans* are good for country.
They troll us in wedding songs.

We say your home is in villages.
They pitch tents in the capital.
We torpedo them with foul water.
They hit back with *Gurvani*.
We spray communal hatred.
They spout the unity of tractors.
We set up barbed wire barricades.
They throw them in the Jamuna.

We call them *Khalistanis*.
They call us Hindu fascists.
We let loose barking *Kanganas*.
They invite her to eat *makki ki roti*..

We plan to call *Jawans* to beat them down.
They say they have a *Jawan* in each house.
We say your shit is all over the border.
They say best place to shit is your Parliament.

We say *Jai Jawan*.
They say *Jai Kisan*.
We fight with batons, tear gas, lathi charges.
They fight with *gehun, sarson, aloo, pyaaz*.
Oh! These *kisans*, what a hindrance to modernity!
What an uncouth loud mouth crowd,
Such a spanner in the corruption wheel!

Note:
*Mandi*: Local wholesale markets
*Gurvani*: The *Guru Granth Sahib*, holy scripture of the Sikh community
*Khalistanis*: An unsuccessful effort to establish the rule of the Sikhs
Kangana: A virulent propagator of the Hinduthwa creed
*Jai Jawan, Jai Kisan*: "Hail soldiers, Hail farmers" was a slogan India adopted
for some time. Now, *Jai Kisan* is almost a forgotten slogan
*Gehun, Sarson, Aloo, Pyaaz* : Wheat, Mustard, Potato, Onions

## THREE PELLETS AND A CRADLE

biscuit

a pellet
hit her small palm
that clutched
a half eaten biscuit.
she broke into a rasping wail
"bikoot mama bikoot"
the biscuit fell to the ground
near her, near her mamma.


mamma

a pellet
hit her left breast
that smelt of milk.
a fount of blood spurted
all over her baby and
soaked a biscuit on the ground.


eye

a pellet
hit Hiba's right eye
in the corner where tear ducts end.
blood and translucent
pieces of flesh erupted

before her eye was covered by her palm.
as the biscuit left her hand
and she fell from mamma's grip
and mamma fell, her face a sieve,
she cried, "eye mamma my eye!"

A SERIES IN 4 EPISODES

## Episode 1

a regiment of old people,
more bones than flesh,
are thrown into an army truck.
to be unloaded in the woods
near some godforsaken border.
but, a fierce debate breaks out
whether they should be blinded or not.
orders are awaited from the capital city.

## Episode 2

a burst of pellets perforate
a sieve on a snow girl's face.
she is blindly seeking the way to her house
when a newsman captures her image.
next day, she appears on media
as a "stone pelter who strayed into
rolls of concertina wire."
the stones in her bag
are being counted.

## Episode 3

the level of the river is raised to 142.
42 more villages get submerged.

42000 tribals and as many trees drown.
a tourist guide invites tourists to the dam
to watch the spectacle of the rising water.
"visit the world's tallest statue
called freedom statue nearby",
cry out the tourism pamphlets and louts.


## Episode 4

a man made object hurls into space
aiming to tickle the moon's shiny skin.
entire nation waits with bated breath
as the lander begins its descent.
the country loses contact with
the lander, the land and the landless.

Note:
Lander: The Indian vehicle that landed on the moon

## SOME PIOUS DEEDS

While razing the house of a Muslim family
and setting them on fire with kerosene
the man was thinking of the Buddhist monastery
he planned to visit in Bhutan.
It was his long drawn wish to meditate
on the mountains where the air was thin.

Meanwhile, the wails of the hapless family
floated back to his ears and he grew
furious at his reveries being disturbed.
He started kicking the bodies before him
trying hard to silence even the whimpers.

When their cries had ceased and the
house was fully razed, he returned to his
pious thoughts about offering a *chadar*
at the *Ajmer Darga* and lighting candles
at the altar of the *Velankanni Church*.

By then a few adolescent lads had started
raising the prayer cries of *Allahu Akbar*.
Raising his baton and crying *Har har Mahadev*
he rushed to their midst, bashing a few skulls.
A stone was flung at him and he raised his pistol
and fired into the crowd with an *Om* on his lips.

Note:

*Chadar*: an offering to this Muslim shrine
*Vellankanni*: Christian church where the virgin is worshipped
*Allahu Akbar, Har Har Mahadev*: War cries of the Muslims and Hindus
Om: Basic chant of the Savarna Hindus

## THE SOMNAMBULIST

Not that I sleep and walk or walk and sleep
or read and sleep or sleep and read,
not that my head nods when a tractor collides headlong
with a police van parked beyond barbed wire,
not that I stand outside a tent and peep on a *langar*
where slogans and rotis roast on a large griddle

Treat me as a thieving political somnambulist, I don't mind.
Time was when I walked in sleep to God's workshop and
apprenticed for melting metal for his crosses and swords.
Time was when I walked in sleep to explosive war fronts
and helped in loading the shells in the long range guns.
Time was when I walked in sleep to the guerilla jungles
and raped , in sleep, many girls for the victorious nation

See, I  used to be  a somnambulist and a photo journalist,
many  fashion magazines published my sodomy images.

But, tonight I walk the sleep the walk
along  the arterial avenues of a sacked city
and charter a yellow submarine like a yellow JCB
and yellow flash through the winter night so foggy
and leave in its wake an assortment of sand stones
industrial complexes warehouses excavators extractors
rushing tumbling gobbling crashing cart wheeling
till the transformer screeches to a halt in front of
the seat of power around a round dining table

where human meat is served in intercontinental cuisines
the chewing slurping swallowing belching farting
so loud that I wake up, a poor somnambulist,
in an ox-driven wooden rubber rimmed bullock cart.

Note:
*Langar:* Community kitchen, efficiently used during the farmers' struggle

## Minnal Maniyan

Minnal Maniyan is a millenium fly
who got his super power from a
mosquito grid. He grew double his
size, dived from mosque minarets
and vomited blue stuff over food.
He was a techie trained in a-history.

His rival was a lean fly named Minnal Maniac
also born of the same grid
and also a techie.
His routine food was
gunpowder on which he puked blue acid.

They were friends till their girl friends
told them that one Minnal was bad
enough for the floundering nation.
This grew to a full scale war and they created
much collateral damage.

The Government finally appealed to the US
who sent two fighter planes.
The Marines captured the Third World flies
and took them to Hollywood where
Marvel Comics sentenced them to death
for plagiarism.

They were roasted in two
parallel electric grills.

Note: Motto: Grid you are and to grid you shall return

## MULLAI AND PALAI

The river in my village is named Mulla.
In my language, it denotes the Jasmine.
In Tamil, it denotes a pastoral tract.
My village was fragrant with the scent of Jasmine.
Every plant, every animal every man was fragrant with the flower.
Boat travellers exclaimed when the boat approached our village
"Here is the fragrant land, the land of prosperity, of peace."

One day, the morning bathers smelled blood.
A mist of blood hung over the water, the air grew thick
with the smell of blood.
Then the bodies came floating, hundreds of them,
slashed, speared and mutilated, turning putrid, oozing
with fluids, disintegrating.
Waters running thick with the sap of dead wood.

We villages fled from the village to Palai land
devoid of trees but escaping death.
We toiled on the arid soil, blood turning to sweat.
longing for the Mulla land we had lost,
singing no songs, writing no poems, loving no one,
till a hundred years passed and the first drop of rain
fell on the land instantly turning to vapour.

More drops fell and it became a torrent
till it became a timeless rain.
A fresh stream flowed along the Palai land
and the earth began to smell of Mulla, the Jasmine.

Note: Palai Land – arid land | Mulla Land – fertile land

## RETURN OF THE SEEDS

Finally we return to the
lukewarm water in the tub
where yesterday's sun has set.

Finally we return to the
warmth of our love's womb
where god created a universe.

We return to the music of the orbs
the swimming diving flesh
the clash of arms
cry of the wounded
crawl of the maimed
where we meet like maggots
on the bodies of dead loves.

Finally we return to
what was eternal
but as ephemeral
as a beetle wing.

We return to
the hesitant touch
the erring grope
the hurried kiss
sowing seeds in
sunflower mouths.

# THE LUMINOUS SEED

Descended a luminous egg from the skies
glittering with strands of silver
light as a lover's whisper
glowing with reminiscences
moist with longing.

Tried to touch her, she shied away,
tried to hold her, she was slippery
as a soul.

Who are you, bright spore from the stars?
I asked.
She retorted (with a touch of resentment)
don't you recognize me, you, with the sweet tongue?
I came sailing on a favorable wind
over a vast bloody ocean and a choppy sea
leaping over an emerald island
sailing sailing  in my urge to see you
I am your souls's seed, your balmy lover,
dying to sprout in you.

With a cry of recognition, I lunged at her
to trap her in my lifeline, but she
slipped out through the fate line.
she was gone in a flash.
I looked for her in vain
but, far away I heard her

laughter growing faint
as she sailed on sailed on
sailed on
away
from
me.

# WHERE, IN WHAT FORM, SHALL WE MEET AGAIN?

Where, in what form, shall we meet again?
I asked.
You as a baby girl, me cuddling you.

Where, in what form, shall we meet again?
She asked.
You as a lake, me the hill reflected in you.

Where, in what form, shall we meet again?
I asked.
You as an open wound, me the gauze bandage.

Where, in what form, shall we meet again?
She asked.
You as a gun, me the bullet.

Where, in what form, shall we meet again?
I asked.
You as petrol, me as kerosene,
making a molotov cocktail.

Where, in what form, shall we meet again?
She asked.
You as a book of verses, me the words.

Where, in what form, will you two meet again?
The BBC reporter asked.
We spoke in unison.
As lame parrots, blind squirrels,
as worms making love in ditches.

## MY TEA

My tea awaits her
in two railway stations
two days a week.
My tea vends itself
only to her.

Thursday afternoons,
my tea awaits her anxiously,
hot in its can, hot to touch,
with sputtering heart
for her to board the train.
My tea seeks her out.
My tea goes to her.
My tea vends itself to her.
My tea makes many trips to her.
She doesn't buy.

After she alights, my tea
grows cold and throws
itself into the river.

On Saturday mornings,
my tea again awaits her,
heart pumping, sweating.
My tea offers itself to her
till she gets down and
my tea grows cold and
throws itself into the river.

My tea loves her
and dies for her
every week.
She doesn't notice
his emotions
and the heart
that pumps hard.
She doesn't know
of his weekly death.

She sips the hot tea
and throws away
the plastic cup.

# A COUPLE BURNING FROM LOVE
*two match sticks burning together*

A flame is a living picture
of a force of energy
that is neither created nor destroyed.
Can love be energy too
that's ever present in a person
never being born nor dead?

See the picture carefully.
A couple is burning
at their tips now
set alight from top to bottom.
One's face is tilted in the heat
as if to kiss the other
even in death.

As the flame engulfs them
they will twist around each other
in throes of ecstasy till
the heads tumble one by one
into an ashen world
devoid of love.

What could be the last words
the match heads spoke
before succumbing to
the energy of love
that is never created nor destroyed
but is ever present.
In what language do the dying
express love?

## LAST LOVE

When you are at the edge
and gleaming cars pass by
you select one driven by a girl
to leap under its tires.

Now, there is her car
and there is not.
No gleaming cars pass by.
There is no road but a huge canal.
You watch a bloated torso float by.

Now, you are at the edge
and rotten bodies pass by
ghost ships reeking of the sea.
someone calls out your name!

A huge flare on the other bank
and burning women jump in.
the blood river licks your feet
chocked with bodies.

You board a burning ship
and sail away in the gloom.
On its mast is crucified
your last love.

## BREAK UP

It took me many years to realize
that break ups were unlike break downs.
It was not merely a linguistic error
but also a revamping of defiant parts.

Being slow in the brain, I went through
ten plus one break ups to learn that
they are tougher than ten break downs
which could be quantified as battery failures,
bad fuel economy, flat tires, rusting, faulty
break system, poor alignment and overheating.

In a break up, however, the cause is inevitably
loss of alignment of aspirations, cardiac overheating,
abrupt discovery of convenient alternatives,
bad combustion of feelings, failure in accelerating,
miscommunication over far distances
and the absence of skin, flesh and blood.

The solution is not to drive or love.
Or, identifying and fixing  a good workshop.
Though it is doubtful whether a workshop
exists for a break up. Mostly one ends up
adding it to a heap of sentimental scrap.

# THE MORTUARY WARS

They say they heard heated exchange of words
in the male mortuary wards.
Actually the cadavers were confused about
the number of them dead.
Each time a roll call was done
an extra body turned up.

They say they saw a march of torches
to the female mortuary wards
where the same confusion prevailed.
Each new body that turned up
was more mutilated and rotten than the earlier one.

They say they saw huge shadows clashing.
What they did not notice was that
the attackers were getting it in their ass.
Out had come the fearsome choppers,
knives, cutters, peelers and slicers
that left the male corpses with no sex.
Some enterprising ladies stashed away pricks
to be sold as dildos in the flea market.

They say they thought it was
the end of the mortuary wars.
But, the gender war was just hotting up.


One day, a stray sexless tsunami wave
carried them away to the sea
where famished sharks waited for them.

## SUNSET RAPE  IN LANGUID HILLS

After the rape, the bamboos didn't resume
their moaning music.
After the rape, the rapist walked to the river
to wash his genitals.

The raped lay in the slush, flowers scattered around her,
the sparrows silent in the bamboos.
The sun slowly went down behind the gloomy hills,
setting fire to her pubis and the river.

The rapist surely noted the silence of the dusk
hooting once or twice to mimic a scream.
The echoes stayed in the hills, the wind went dumb
and the skies turned deaf as the silent river.

When the raped rose up and gathered her clothes
and walked to the river to wash her wound,
the chirps of a hundred sparrows suddenly filled the air
and the creaking bamboos cried out with the roar of the wind.

The river ran with her blood, not the dead sun's,
and the blood would never stop from her mashed womb.

Later, as she limped home to an unlit hearth
and a crying baby and a dying mother,
the blood streamed along her thighs and wet her feet.

The rapist followed her lazily, biting into a fruit,
his eyes set on the trail of blood till THE END.

Note: From the anthology, *A Strange Place Other Than Earlobes*

# WHY DID YOU RAPE ME?

The glare of the sun woke me up.
I yawned when her head hid the sun.
She had switched off the AC.
So, things were quiet. She was quiet.
As in ghost films, a tap dripped on the tub.
A house pigeon crooned outside.
Traffic rumbled vaguely on Mission Street.
My belly rumbled. I was hungry.

Like a gunshot going off, she asked,
"Why did you rape me last night?"

She showed me. She was naked.
I counted. There were thirty three.
I noted down on a scrap book.
Bites on her nipples – four.
Bites on her lips – three.
Strangulation marks on her throat – one
Nail marks on her face – two.
Scratches on her behind – four.
Spank marks – six.
Finger marks on her thighs – four.
Rope marks on her wrists – two.
Rope marks on her ankles – two.
Miscellaneous – four.

"Why did you rape me?"
Her question, like a gunshot again.

Her palm gripped my limp prick.
"Why did you tie me up and rape me?"

Room 201 grew warm. I was sweating.
We made love twice during the day.
Twice in the night.
She snored slightly as I spooned her.
We were the happiest lovers on earth.
I slept with the scent of her hair in my cells.

Her grip on my prick grew harder.
I remembered her cries…
Stop Stop. Don't hurt me!
She brought her face down and bit my lips.
I saw the blood on her lips.
Her teeth smeared with blood.
Her tongue dripping blood.
She asked again, "Why?"

I remember growing hard
before I slipped into darkness.

# END OF THE SEX WAR

A man is a pen is a gun
said the hu-man male
mans-plaining-things
to a hu-man female.

What went wrong
what went wrong
queried their quivering organs.
Oh these hu-mans
with their trash bags full
of theories and resolutions!

Has a clit ever read Anais Nin?
Has a prick ever skimmed through
Fanny Hill?

Wasn't she just howling
quotes from Second Sex?
Wasn't he just yelling
revolution is a mass orgy
as they both came in unison?

Now they are fighting
over -O-R-G-A-S-M
as it works for her
and for him.!

Or, we thought so.
Their duel comes to nought.

Aiow! This is worse!
The witch is now
making tea for him.
The prick is reading
vaginal monologues.

Anais Nin — famous writer known for some erotica
Fanny Hill — a famous erotic book
Second Sex — monumental book by Simone de Beauvoir on the female
gender

## MS TINY TITS

Once, two small tits and a tipless prick
met in a lonely deserted moonlit night
in a bed decorated with wild flowers.

The prick tore the spongy bra apart
and began to suck the small tits hungrily.
But, the prick's teeth were failing in it
as the tits were too tiny to grip.

The tipless prick asked the tits
why are you so horribly tiny.
The tits replied, we were being
manhandled so many times
that we couldn't get a chance
to grow since our birth.

Seeing the prick's predicament,
Ms Tiny Tits pushed the prick
on the bed and peeling down the jeans
was about to take it  in her mouth when
she was shocked seeing the wound
where the tip should have been.

When Tiny Tits asked the tipless prick
what misfortune befell its tip,
the impudent unrepentant  prick said
I am one of the habitual predators
who claws tits every now and then.
In my last encounter with a stubborn
 savage tit the witch mauled me so bad
 and bit off the tip in revenge.

## SHE AND SHEMALE

The screen in blue brilliance
flaring up with cuts and pans,
the monitor emitting sepia smoke,
her lips on my nips angling deep
teeth jamming like wire cutter jaws.

I touch her booboos as the
shemale looks up with a
virginal smile which infects the one
who navigates down my belly with her tongue.
I fondle the shemale's booboos, lost in his/her saintly smile.

From the shemale's booboos I row down as her lips
sail to my underbelly.
The shemale smiles and directs
me to his/her erect phalloos
while she does a mirror act.

The shemale's throboos is in my mouth as she starts
chewing me whole. I'm sucked into a swirlpool.
Shemale screams and she screams as they die the little death.

In a splash, he/she stands in the glory of the blue white
tangerine glow of the tube.

Her booboos and the shemale's phalloos do a victory
jig crying out in xstacy as the shemale moves closer to the
camera in full splendor of his/her twin genders and
merges with the one viewing her,

Me merging with her and him/her to vanish without history.

Note: In most porn flicks, a Shemale is an extremely beautiful woman
with well developed breasts but with a penis in place of vagina
The poem is built around this. Consider that a male is watching as hemale porn
with his female lover. At the end, there is a total merger of the three

## ODE TO AN UNSENDING GIRL

The wierdest girl I know is the unsending girl.
You guessed right, I know many girls,
 the dreamy girl, the running girl, the hard working girl,
the boozing girl, the worshipping girl, the kick boxing girl,
the sloganeering girl, the stone throwing girl, the teaching
girl,
the farming girl, the architecture girl, the IT girl, the
fornicating girl,
the lesbian girl, the army girl, the smelly girl, the body
selling girl.

This one, I have known her for many years.
Her copy pasted profile is alluring.
I think it's Keira or Anne.

I don't know much about hoogliwood.
nor do I know anything about her
because she is the unsending girl.

Imagine this conversation.

me: what do I call you, sweet? I didn't get your name.
she: unsends a sent message.

me: which devilforsaken place are you from?
she: unsends a sent message.

me: are you a major?
she: unsends a sent message.
me: what are you, an executive, bartender, vice-president, janitor, hooker?
she: unsends a sent message.

me: can we have a blind date?
she: unsends a sent message.

me: (hums) chumma chumma de de….
she: fuck off you desi maggot!

# A DESPERATE STRAIGHT MAN'S LAMENT

You shiver like a nun
when I touch you!
*(have you ever touched a nun? the critic asks.*
*I go mute!)*

You wobble like a sanyasin
when I blow air on your earlobe.
*(have you ever blown a storm on  an earlobe? the critic asks.*
*I go mute!)*

You grow hot and flush like a strict school mistress
when I run my nose through your shampooed hair.
*(have you ever smelled the shampoo on a school mistress? the critic asks.*
*I go mute!)*

Your eyes turn into embers like a political activist
when I gaze intently into your eyes, boring deep.
*(have you ever gazed into the eyes of a political activist? the critic asks.*
*I go mute!)*

You punch me in a flash like a boxer
when I feel the smoothness of your varnished nails.
*(have you ever felt the nails of a boxer? the critic asks.*
*I go mute!)*

You crush the hard disk of my system or my phone
when I write a poem about your poem about my poem.

*(have you ever written a poem about a poet? the critic asks.*
*I go mute!)*

You jab *your knee into* my groin and my balls
when I plant a soft kiss on your lips, my love!
*(have you ever kissed the woman you love? the critic asks.*
*I go mute!)*

I  say
love your love and your love and your love etc.
love your woman and your woman and your woman etc.
Squared, Cubed, Quartic(ed*)*
Etc.

## LOVE IN THE TIME OF THE KARUNA VIRUS

No one bothered till the Karuna virus caught the police
chanting the Hindu god's name and chasing Muhammedans
along with the mobs. The virus had its miraculous debut in
Shaheen Bagh when one by one the policemen stopped in their
tracks and lowered the batons. The ones demolishing the Masjids
stopped work and came down as if nothing ever happened.

Some army men who went back to Kashmir, carried the virus
with them and the torture camps were suddenly abandoned.
The army returned to the bases. Schools reopened. Internet was
established in full. Streets were filled with singing dancing people.

The spread of the Karuna virus was swift.
It swept across Assam and the North East.
The detention camps were evacuated  and people streamed out in joy.

The virus entered China and the Uyghur Muslims
were sent back to families
from the concentration camps.
Pro-democracy protesters were let out of jail.
Same good news awaited the Rohingyas in Myanmar.

North Korea ended their sham communism.
By the banks of the Amazon
forests, the indigenous people were returned the forests.
The wall between
Mexico and the US was demolished.

US brought back all its marines from
Syria, Iraq and Aghanistan.
Saudi Arabia banned capital punishment.
In Iran, the dissenters were released.
Aboriginal rights were accepted in Australia.
The natives got their dues in the US.
Israeli troops withdrew from Palestine.
All passports and visa restrictions were rendered invalid globally.

The symptoms of the Karuna vius were noticeable everywhere.
People were happy.
unburdened by wars, the governments spent more on food and culture.
Happy couples roamed the streets in the cities and the villages
freely, no one bothered them.
No one watched anyone kissing. Anyone hugging.

Me and my beloved entered the bamboo groves in the western ghats
and lay on the ground making love to the rhythm of the creaking trunks.
A snake slithered past our bodies. A bird pecked at her nipples.
Ants scurried along my spine.
A hundred fireflies lit up our dance of love.
A rain of Karuna fell on us.

## A JATKA IN THE NIGHT

To reach Sheshadri's clinic, one had to catch a
Jatka, the only one at the junction, in an age when
there were no cabs or scooters or buses.

The Jatka was an improvement on the bullock cart,
horse driven and with rubberized wheels. It flew along
the roads of Chittur which were not many so to say.
A road led to Pollachi, another to Palakkad and another to
Trissur.

The Jatka had a sack of grass and grain hung below
for the horse to leisurely chew on.
One day, the Jatka carried my cousin to the clinic
and brought her back dead.
The jingles of the Jatka later reminded me of her golden anklets.

The Jatka itself died when the first cab appeared
at the junction. It stood abandoned at the junction
till the owner died. The horse that was set free roamed the streets
for some time before disappearing towards the hills.

Later, more cabs came and three-wheelers too and the
town got busy decorating itself with many towers and
concrete structures in its hurry to be a city. More people
thronged the boulevards, malls and multiplexes that came
up. Buses plied over crowded. Metro trains passed under
the city. A murder a day became common. Rapes too.

One day, I reached the town by a late bus and found no transport to my village. Then I heard a call, freezing my senses, " Saar, where to, sir?" The Jatka stood there freshly painted and the horse well fed and healthy. The Jatka man stood smoking a beedi as if he had never died. Disbelievingly, I boarded the Jatka that left me near my house near a bamboo grove and four coconuts trees in a row. When I looked up from my wallet to pay him, I found no Jatka there. It had vanished leaving me terrified.

Even now, on new moon nights when the traffic dies down, I often hear the jingles of the horse and its trots and the swear words that the Jatka man threw at the horse. It would immediately be drowned by an ambulance wail carrying Corona dead people to the crematorium...

## TWO COVID-19 VIRUSES MEET ALBERT CAMUS

The world was calm now. And silent.
Only the birds chirped tweeted sang cawed.
Only the animals barked mewed mooed growled.
Only the river gurgled.
Only the sky thundered.
Only the fires crackled.

Two covid-19 teenage viruses walked around the city
assessing the damage. On Route vers l'ouest, they found
mansions with cars parked in front and little gardens.
Four dogs ran out of the house dragging a well dressed
woman and a naked man. It was the posh area of the city
and in house after house dogs feasted.

On Route Vers le nord, that led to the fields, unharvested paddy
lay in the fields. That was the operational area of the rodents,
snakes and the jackals. On Route vers l'est, that led to the offices,
the road lay thick with the police, applicants, clerks, officers and
mounds of paper. The vultures landed on them and tore away
the flesh.  It was a mass of rotting flesh, blood, hair and
official communiqué.

On Route vers le sud that led to the river, peacocks danced on
the road. From the two theatres that showed no films, super stars
grinned from posters. Weeds were slowly climbing up the
courtyards of the college and the schools. The grounds were
covered with bodies , furniture, lab instruments and aprons.

The teenage viruses reached the river and sat holding hands.
Being young, they were in love and being idealistic a tad bit
sad about the end of humans.

They then spied a human in a trench coat and trousers angling for
fish  on the bank. He smoked a pipe and chuckled while he spoke
to the fishes. The adolescent viruses approached him and asked,
"Who are you sir, how come you are in one piece when
all humans are dead all over the world?"

The man chuckled again and retorted, "I am Camus
and I wrote a novel 'The Plague' long back. I wrote that the city
was happy, life went on, but the plague bacillus never dies or
disappears for good. It can lie dormant for years and years
in bedrooms, cellars, trunks and bookshelves and perhaps the day
would come when it roused up its rats again and sent them
into a happy city.  You are those rats now and you are the plague."

The Gen X viruses who could barely understand him, watched
as Camus gathered his things and made his way up stream with
fishing rods, bait and the day's catch, whistling to himself.

Note: From the last lines of the novel, *The Plague*

## PATHOLOGY OF A RAINBOW

Today on the pathologist's table
lay a rainbow
twisted and maimed
tongue seeking air.

I, as the pathologist,
dictated notes.
Death by strangulation
after rape.

With a scalpel
I slit open the body
along the contours
colour by colour.

Violet ashened by shock
indigo grafted on soiled blue
irreparably grilled by
green yellowed by a paste of
orange peels and red dust
of a planet which had died
a million years ago
from want of oxygen.

I signed the report that said
to determine the cause of death
the pathologist needs more colours,

drained from dead flowers, trees,
animal sap, volcanic ash, coral reefs,
crayons and a few broken bangles.

When I went out into the sunshine,
I heard a rumble and
the wail of suffocated rainbows.

## CONTEMPORARY BACTERIA

The docs are worrying too much.
They detect new bacteria inside me
every day.
I have seen images of bacteria
unimaginatively sketched by
newspaper artists.
Some look wooly some curly
some slimy and some with gnarling teeth.

I am almost tempted to make one my pet.
It may win at a pet show next year.
Alas! My docs kill one as soon as
they spot one. But like Ravan's head,
a new one sprouts in its place.

They do not know that they are clever
one-cell wonders who like Rajni Kant
can evade any cut blow shot or bombardment.
This time I demanded - show them to me.
I peered through the scope and and
found to my joy a hundred bacteria in congregation.

They were like Solomon's Stones
brilliant sizzling and sun worshiping.
I raised my face and whooped.
I ran a lap around the lab.
The docs could hardly catch up.

I cried, "They are a hundred contemporary bacteria
and I add my number to them."
Before they restrained me, I plummeted
down the scope.
The docs looked again and saw
to their dismay
hundred and one contemporary bacteria
in the Garden of Hades who spoke
with colours pictures and memory ripples.

## DEATH OF AN INFLAMMABLE WOMAN

She was found still emitting smoke.
Her smudgy edges were yellow
from the last lick of flame.
Along with the limbs,
the heart that was wrenched out
still kept pumping scalding blood.

Drained inflammable spirit
hung around her like a shroud.
To the detective
scrapping burnt skin from the molten asphalt, she said
Please love me.
To the ambulance driver
transporting her cooked flesh to the mortuary, she said
Please love me.
To the pathologist
who was trying to put together a coherent dish, she said
Please love me.
To the crematorium operator
who pushed her dough into the oven, she said
Please love me.
To the river
which carried her left overs to her home land, she said
Please love me.

Suicide bombers don't leave suicide notes.
They leave the smell of incinerated carbon
roasted dna and a charred dream.

# MANY A TIME

Believe me!
You don't worry!
I am exceptionally good at farewells.

Many a time
I have been a pseudo leather shoe
left on a rail terminus
while my pair continued to travel.

Many a time
I have been a crushed can of beer
thrown out of a bus
while a dozen journeyed on in a pack.

Many a time
I have been a syllable
left on a writer's pad
while the rest formed new symbols.

Many a time
I am just an empty shell
left on a beach
in craters formed in sand.

Believe me!
I am exceptionally good
at farewells.
I don't shed precious tears,
just blood.

## NARCISSUS DOES THE MIRROR ACT

In a river mirror/mirror river, I am rippled
shredded and strewn by rock faces.

In a sea  mirror/mirror sea, I am spiked
skewered and sunk by shark teeth.

In a pool mirror/mirror pool, I am gobbled
pebbled  and frothed by shagging pricks.

In a room mirror/mirror room, I am denuded
pricked and buggered by shadow lights.

In an eye mirror/mirror eye, I am miniaturized
tinied by flies and circled by organic orbits.

In a mirror mirror/mirror mirror, I am I-ed and eyed
I eye / eye I.

## On Photography
*Remembering Susan Sontag*

A camera has three eyes. One gazes at the object.
One, burrows into the object.
One, inside itself.

The first eye makes eye contact with the eye of the object.
The second eye touches the eye inside the object .
And they hesitate like two lovers about to mate.
The third eye is the witness.
It reaches inside the camera and drags out that image
That is the truest representation.

Poetry happens when
All six eyes write each other.
Poetry is the camera, the object and the image,
All rolled into One.

## Sound Bites

One day, I get a sound clip
with one word chanted ten times.
My name in ten languages without script.

It's her voice from the stratosphere
from the ozone layer from space
rom beyond space beyond some.

Cosmic debris of a long dead star
My name my name my name
In her voice of honeyed love
That settles on me like a rich thick
Fog of winter mist pollen star dust.

A sound clip is a tricky matter
Devoid of mass energy volume
But it's dense with gravity
A magnetic storm on a far away planet
It pulls me in a whorl in a weird whirl
To the depths she inhabits now
Voice voice sound sound echo echo
Her lungs, her heaving bosom, her voice chords.

See, she has been dead for a hundred years
yet I float in her sadness
like a pickled embryo.

## THE FIRST SYLLABLE

How do you call her in your bhasha*language?
Fondling her poossy lovingly, I asked.
She blushed and a flush spread on her.
With the flush, her poossy too blushed.
Take it from me –
The scarlet of a poossy is what is scarlet.


She covered her face in shame and
blurted out a word.
But, that's a poovu*/flower, I said.
That's fine. Call her so.
So, I called her poossy a poovu*.


Her poossy flooded like never before,
became a lake, a sea, a storm,
a thundercloud, a howl.
a flood of menstrual blood.


Bobbing up and down on the sea of blood
she said, baptize me in your language,
make me write your word.

I became her Guru,
her finger, the stylus

her thigh, the white sand.
I dipped her finger in the blood
and made her write the first syllable.
Poo..*

Note: Writing the first syllable is an important ritual in Kerala. It marks the beginning of education. Usually, it starts by writing Hari, the name of Lord Vishnu. Here, the syllable used is Poo which is the first syllable of the word Pooru which is slang for vagina like Pussy/Poossy is. Poo can also be the first syllable for Poovu* which means a flower

## THE EX-COMMUNISTS OR EXORCISED COMMUNISTS, A FARCE

As the great graveyard of martyrs was being auctioned,
there were very few takers, except a global guy.
He was hailed as a messaih opening new vistas of jobs
and opportunities adding to the labour class numbers.

This is class war, extolled the local leader, who had
just been cured of a bout of whooping cough.
More speakers arrived explaining why the graveyard was
just a piece of property on which a Mall could be built.
35000 sq feet, hundreds of employees, the entire township
could be absorbed as labour class.

In the night, a few martyrs came out of their graves
and sat on the few tombstones around. "Where do we
go when the mall is built? Where do we hang around
in revolutionary spirit?" A hot-blooded young spirit
said, "Comrades, this is our graveyard. a paradise on
earth for the martyrs of the cause. We should resist in
true revolutionary fashion as we resisted the landlords."

But, the earth movers came and dug up all the graves
and deposited the bones and skulls in a corner.
Some martyr spirits took to flight, some stayed put, waiting
for the building work to start in right ernest and vigour.

In the sprawling mall, customers sometimes heard suppressed

groans and exasperated cries from locked rooms.
And faint sounds of marching boots and firearms spitting fire.
A sudden staccato of machine gun fire sometimes screamed
across the mall, sending customers and staff scampering.

An ex-communist exorcist was pressed into service. All
his attempts to shoo away the martyr spirits failed.
Finally, a greenhorn marketing executive got a flash of wisdom.
"Let's rename the Mall as The Commune, comrades."

The ploy worked. The martyr spirits were appeased.
The young guy won a 10% discount coupon on all goods sold.
The martyrs slumbered in air conditioned comfort.

# THE RUSSIAN PREDATOR

Once again, there is blood on Neruda's streets.

Once again, there are those sickening images
of mothers grieving,
of families looking for their bread winners,
of little girls picking blood splattered flowers,
of airplanes bombing apartments and schools.

Once again, war photos will fill pages.
One will get the Pulitzer prize.
Many will get Russian gallantry awards.

The language of Dostoesky, Tolstoy,
Pushkin, Chekhov, Gorky and Bulgakov
will once again invade the poor language of Ukraine.

Once again, a nation of nation-less people
will be born.

A Russian predator is on the prowl.

## OBITUARY TO A MAN IN HURRY

I found the quick silver Man
Light footed in a Hurry
Moving so like a Flash
I could hardly Match.

He accelerated so Fast
He left things Behind
He rushed ahead ten Paces
As I walked behind in the Corridor
Trying not to trample On
The things that spilled Out.

Shirts, drawer strings, marbles, Flowers,
Sheets, socks, condoms, Pens,
Books, rum bottles, Staplers,
Flower vases, openers, Clippers,
A dictionary, two Thesauruses,
An anthology of Poems.

I jumped over them like a steeple Chaser
As he moved fast to his Cab
He by then dragged behind an empty Strolley.

I watched at the Airport
As he walked towards his Flight
Leaving behind the Strolley
I could see the wind whipping off his Shirt
I saw him entering the plane Naked.

Learned later that a man by that Name
Never got off that Flight.
On the job is Google Search.
Looking for him among the Clouds.
Lit up by an occasional Comet.

# THE FALLEN CONDOM — A CONDOMPORARY MUSICAL TRAGEDY

Look at me,
a used condom
now on a busy road
where MRF tyres crunch me to tar.
(MRF tyres advt plays)

Once I felt smooth and wet,
fragrant like an emperor's garden
with a rare fruit flavor
good to sniff, good to savour
(Tootie Frootie advt plays)

Flexible and filling
not a size too large
coming in small large and extra large
depending on the nationality.
(Sare jahan se acha (Our country is the best) song plays)

I never rip or tear
in the midst of severe ecstasy
or burst like a China made rubber
leading to scandals and abortions.
(Chinese cultural revolution song plays)

It was a proud moment
to be unsheathed in a BMW interior

to adorn a ten incher monster
in a non-consensual scenario.
(Mein khiladi Tu anari (Am a veteran, you an innocent) song plays)

Alas! Alas! He blew up to a full footer
and I burst toottar foottar,
in disgust was the window slid open
and me the Condom King flung on NH 47.
(Malayalam song Njan Njan Njan enna bhaavangale (Ego ego ego)
song plays)

Learn from my plight, oh passerby!
Vanity is evil, Vanity is devil.
Residing in Chinese, Indian or French brands,
now I am but a rotten skin, sadly deathless
on this highway paved with discarded condoms.
(Malayalam song 'Veena poove' (Fallen flower) plays.)

## ODE TO BLACK HOLES

All holes are not
shaped like holes
or round holes.

Some are square
some oval
some triangular
some hexagonal.

Some are long
some wide
some are tubular
some come with webs.

Some come with glue
some taste like lichis
some like wine.

All holes are holes
or no hole is a hole.
A hole is actually a non-hole.
Rarely are they wholly holes
but they are whole when
they end in a hole on
the other end of a hole.

# THE UNBEARABLE YELLOWNESS OF YELLOW DEATHS

Yellow me lives in a mustard yellow
yello house with yellow walls and a
yellow window from which I can see a
yellow road winding its way to a
yellow hill. a yellow tree with
yellow blossoms greet me every
yellow morning. I sleep on a
yellow bed and watch a
yellow sun pouring in through the
yellow foliage. Beyond the casuarinas tress
yellow plumes rise from cremated kids with
yellow bloated faces and yellow eyes.

Yellowest room of this yellow home houses a
yellow serpent who when roused from her
yellow slumber lasting many
yellow centuries, slither into my bed throwing a
yellow coil around me. She hisses, "hey
yellow poet, write with my forked
yellow tongue. Write two
yellow poems at a stroke, one for
yellow me and one for
yellow you." That's when I shed my
yellow skin and become a
yellow phallus stylus pen squirting
yellow ink about yellow deaths of yellow kids.

## DRANYEN

*for Tibetan freedom and the many pleasant days I spent in the Himalaya bar
drinking Chhang from cut glasses in Majnu ka Tila Tibetan colony near Delhi
University*

To begin with
I didn't know what he was playing.
It was shaped like a snake or a snake gourd and
wailed when he ran his fingers up and down its spine.

But I heard some clouds whiplashing the peaks
and the screams of the moon as the sun stabbed
its belly and the heartbeats of a young *chiru*
hanging from the fangs of a speedy red fox.

I knew then
that it was dipped in a pool of sorrow
that lay still in a high valley beyond the snow.

When he finished, the sun had fallen behind the high cliff
and it was time to repay him.
I emptied out my bag and counted the notes and gave them
all to him, the heap.

He smiled and took it and went on his way,
vanishing up the mountain path in a burst of mist.

When I reached home
I found within my bag the dranyen he played
that began to wail on its own.

Note:
Dranyen: A stringed instrument played by Tibetans
Chiru: Tibetan antelope

www.ingramcontent.com/pod-product-compliance
Lightning Source LLC
Chambersburg PA
CBHW051440140726
47987CB00006B/2471